Fantastic Paper Flying Machines

Fantastic Paper Flying Machines

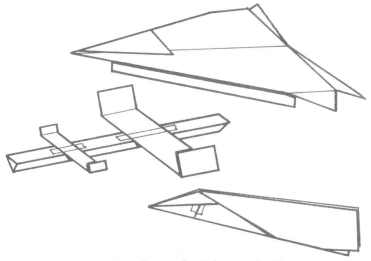

E. Richard Churchill

Illustrated by James Michaels

Sterling Publishing Co., Inc. New York

Library of Congress Cataloging-in-Publication Data

Churchill, E. Richard (Elmer Richard)
    Fantastic paper flying machines / by E. Richard Churchill ;
illustrated by James Michaels.
        p.   cm.
    Includes index.
    ISBN 0-8069-0435-6
    1. Paper airplanes—Juvenile literature.   [1. Paper airplanes.
2. Handicraft.]   I. Michaels, James, ill.   II. Title.
TL778.C484   1994
745.592—dc20   93-44604
                                                                         CIP
                                                                          AC

10   9   8   7   6   5   4   3   2   1

First paperback edition published in 1995 by
Sterling Publishing Company, Inc.
387 Park Avenue South, New York, N.Y. 10016
© 1994 by E. Richard Churchill
Distributed in Canada by Sterling Publishing
% Canadian Manda Group, One Atlantic Avenue, Suite 105
Toronto, Ontario, Canada M6K 3E7
Distributed in Great Britain and Europe by Cassell PLC
Villiers House, 41/47 Strand, London WC2N 5JE, England
Distributed in Australia by Capricorn Link (Australia) Pty Ltd.
P.O. Box 6651, Baulkham Hills, Business Centre, NSW 2153, Australia
Manufactured in the United States of America

Sterling ISBN 0-8069-0435-6 Trade
                0-8069-0436-4 Paper

**For Andrew Sean Churchill, a young man with
a great future**

Contents

Prepare for Takeoff!

To make and fly paper airplanes, all you need is a sheet of paper and a little imagination.

The fantastic paper flying machines in this book come in many shapes. Some are designed for long, straight flights; others are intended to fly short distances and perhaps do a loop or a turn as they fly. In the chapter on *Oddities*, you'll learn how to make some flying machines that aren't airplanes at all!

To construct most of the paper flying machines in this book, notebook paper, typing paper, or computer paper will work perfectly. From time to time you'll need a piece or two of tape. Cellophane tape or masking tape will do the job nicely. Once in a while, one kind of tape is easier to use than the other. When this is so, the instructions will mention the fact. You'll also need a pair of scissors for a bit of cutting on some of the flying machines.

Two airplanes are constructed from file-folder material. You'll also need a chunk of cardboard tubing (the big tubing inside large rolls of gift wrap) for one of the *Oddities*.

Sometimes you'll need a paper clip or two to add to an airplane's nose to give it the proper balance, or "trim" (see page 29).

Anything you need to build these fantastic flying machines should be easy to locate. You won't have to rush off to any store to buy anything.

Folding and flying paper airplanes is fun and exciting. The great thing is that if something goes wrong, all you've lost is a sheet of paper. Don't get upset if an airplane is torn or smashed during a hard landing. Straighten out a mashed nose, tape up a small rip, and fly it again. If your favorite flying machine gets too wrinkled or mashed, just fold another one.

Don't be afraid to experiment. There's no one correct way to fold paper airplanes. After you've built a flying machine the way this book suggests, feel free to make another one, just a little different. Your changes may create an entirely

No flying in the house!

new paper airplane that will fly differently from the original model.

When you fly your paper flying machines, obey a few common-sense safety rules. Don't fly them in a room full of breakable items. Never fly paper airplanes towards another person. You never know exactly where a paper airplane will land.

Several of the flying machines in the book are for outdoor flying only. You'll want to fly many of the others outside. If an airplane lands in the street, don't rush out to rescue it. Even if it gets run over, you can fold a new one in just a minute or so. When an airplane ends up in a tree or on a roof, don't waste time trying to get it down. Make a new airplane, and let the wind blow down the old one some other day.

SMOOTH-SAILING DARTS

1.
Smooth-Sailing Darts

Darts are long, fairly slim paper airplanes that usually have a long, smooth flight. Launch them with a gentle forward flip of the wrist and they'll fly steadily, and for a long distance. If you're into speedy flight, launch your darts fast.

There are many ways to fold *Darts*. As you make the four *Darts* described in this chapter, you'll discover several things about all of them. They're constructed with a series of folds which give them a pointed nose. The layers of paper which build up during the folding give *Darts* a lot of weight in the nose. This heavy nose is partly responsible for their long, steady flights.

The wings on *Darts* are long and slim, and they stay close to the body, or fuselage. Such wings explain the straight flight paths of *Darts*.

Dart I

Begin *Dart I* by folding a sheet of notebook paper, typing paper, or computer paper in half the long way. Crease the fold and then unfold the paper so that it lies flat. With this first fold in place, *Dart I* should look like the drawing shown in Illus. 1.

The two dotted lines in Illus. 1 show where to make your next two folds. Fold over the paper so that the edges come right to the center fold you just made.

Once these folds are in place, your project should look like Illus. 2, where two more dotted lines show where your next

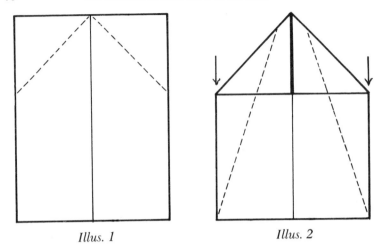

Illus. 1   *Illus. 2*

pair of folds will be. When you make these folds, the two corners or points of paper (indicated by the arrows in Illus. 2) will come right to the center fold.

Tip: Always look ahead to the next drawing before you start folding, so that you can see how your paper flying machine will look once the fold (or folds) you're about to make is (are) in place.

Illus. 3 shows how things will look once the points of paper

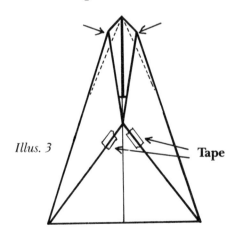

Illus. 3   **Tape**

indicated by the arrows meet at the center crease. Tear off two little pieces of cellophane tape or masking tape and tape these flaps down. You can see the tape in place in Illus. 3. This tape will keep the wings in place as you continue folding.

In Illus. 3 you also see two dotted lines, indicating where to make your next pair of folds. When you make these folds be sure the two points of paper indicated by the arrows come together right at the center fold of *Dart I*. Illus. 4 shows *Dart I* with these folds in place.

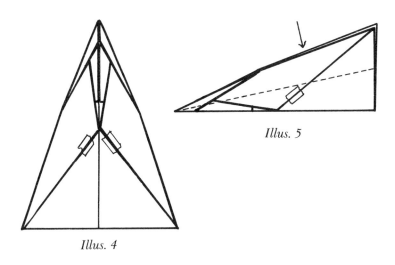

Illus. 5

Illus. 4

Reverse the center fold, and fold *Dart I* in half, so that it looks like the one shown in Illus. 5. This leaves the smooth side of the paper inside the airplane, and all the folded edges will be on the outside.

Check the dotted line shown in Illus. 5. Fold down the side of the plane that's nearer to you along that dotted line. Make this fold so that the edge of the wing indicated by the arrow comes exactly to the bottom of the body (fuselage).

Once you've folded down one wing into place, turn over *Dart I* and fold the second wing in exactly the same way. At this point your airplane should look like Illus. 6.

Now lift the wings you just folded down so that they stick straight out from the fuselage. Hold *Dart I* so that your

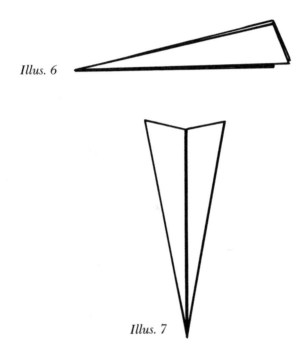

Illus. 6

Illus. 7

thumb and forefinger are right on the little pieces of tape to press the fuselage together. When viewed from the top, your airplane should look exactly like the one shown in Illus. 7.

Launch *Dart I* with a steady forward move with your hand and wrist. This great airplane will take off and fly a long distance in a smooth, steady flight.

Another tip: Sometimes you'll discover that you made a fold that's just a little different from the one shown in the book. For example, back at Illus. 2, your fold may have been a fraction of an inch closer to the nose or farther away from the nose than the fold shown in the drawing. If this happens, your airplane will look just a tiny bit different from the one shown in the book.

Don't worry if this happens. Your airplane will fly just fine. If you can see that a fold starts at a corner, make absolutely certain yours does too. When two pieces of paper are supposed to meet, make sure they do. If a fold angles across part of the airplane, and your fold is a little bit different from the one shown in the drawing, don't worry about it; just try to make your plane look as much as possible like the drawings shown.

Dart II

Begin *Dart II* by folding a sheet of notebook paper, typing paper, or computer paper in half the long way so that it looks like Illus. 8. The dotted line shown on Illus. 8 indicates the first fold you'll make.

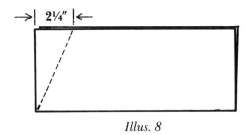

Illus. 8

This fold begins just a little more than 2″ from the corner of the paper. Fold only the top layer towards you. Once this fold is in place, fold the other side of the airplane in exactly the same way.

When these folds are done, *Dart II* can be seen in Illus. 9. Illus. 9 also shows another dotted fold line. When you make this fold begin by folding only the layer of paper nearer you, just as you did for the fold you just finished. Fold over the upper edge of the paper so that it comes exactly to the bottom edge of the little triangle you first folded down.

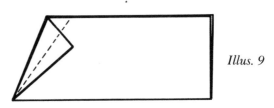

Illus. 9

To be sure you make this fold correctly, check Illus. 10 first. Once you've folded the top layer of paper, fold the other side of the plane in exactly the same way.

Illus. 10

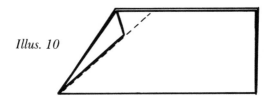

To make the fold shown by the dotted line in Illus. 10, simply fold over the part of the airplane you've just been folding. Fold both sides in exactly the same way, and you should be at Illus. 11.

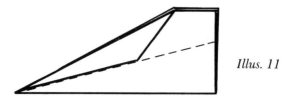

Illus. 11

As you can see from the dotted fold line shown in Illus. 11, your final fold will be made in the same way as the fold you just finished. Fold over the paper one more time. This will bring the top edge of the paper down, so that it's even with the bottom of the fuselage. If the top edge (now the edge of *Dart II*'s wing) ends up a fraction of an inch higher or lower than the bottom of the fuselage, don't worry about it. Your airplane will still fly perfectly. Illus. 12 shows how *Dart II* looks after all this folding.

Illus. 12

Lift the wing nearer to you and stick on a small piece of tape, as shown in Illus. 13, and then do the same for the other wing. Lift both wings so that they extend straight out from the fuselage.

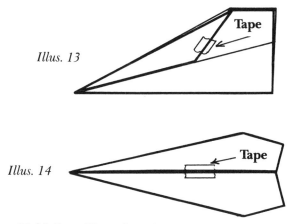

Illus. 13

Illus. 14

Hold *Dart II* so that the wings face up and the fuselage extends down. Pull the wings together and use another little

Wait! Let me help you with that folding.

piece of tape to fasten the wings together. Illus. 14 shows a top view of *Dart II* with this tape in place and ready to fly.

Grasp *Dart II*'s fuselage between your thumb and your forefinger, halfway between its nose and tail. Launch it with a firm forward flip of your hand and wrist.

Dart II will fly a smooth, even flight path for a long distance. Right at the end of its flight, *Dart II*'s nose will rise as it runs out of power and stalls, and then it will come down nose first.

Why do paper airplanes sometimes fly great in one direction and crash when you try to fly them in the opposite direction? Just a slight breeze can make all the difference in the world. Even the draft from an open window may influence the way a paper airplane flies.

Many paper airplanes fly better when they're launched *into* whatever draft or breeze is present.

Dart III

It shouldn't be a surprise that you'll begin this fantastic paper flying machine by folding a sheet of notebook paper or computer paper in half the long way. The next fold you'll make in *Dart III* is shown by the dotted line in Illus. 15.

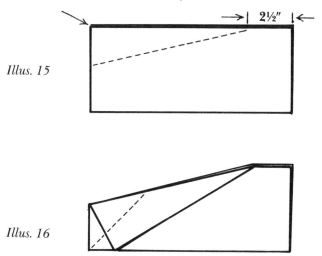

Illus. 15

Illus. 16

Fold the top layer of paper towards you. Begin the fold about 2½″ from the right-hand side of the paper, as shown in Illus. 15. Make certain that the left-hand corner (shown by the arrow in the drawing) comes right to the center fold.

Once you've folded the side nearer to you, make exactly the same fold on the other side of the airplane.

This will bring you to Illus. 16. When you fold along the

dotted line shown in Illus. 16, the front edge will come down right to the center fold (which is also the bottom of the fuselage). Take a quick peek ahead to Illus. 17 to see how

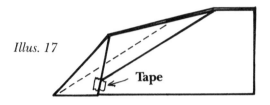

Illus. 17

things look once this fold is in place.

Illus. 17 shows where to place a small bit of tape to help hold things together. Tape the other side of *Dart III* in the same way.

The dotted line in Illus. 17 shows where to fold next. Make this fold on *both* wings. Once this fold is finished, *Dart III* looks pretty much like the one shown in Illus. 18.

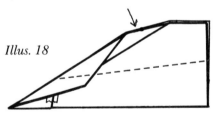

Illus. 18

Now for your final fold. Study the dotted fold line shown in Illus. 18 before you make this fold. Note that it angles *up- wards* as the fold gets nearer to the airplane's tail. Also notice that this fold begins about 1½″ in back of the nose. Fold carefully and crease the material firmly, since you'll be fold- ing a number of layers of paper.

When this fold is in place, the edge of the wing (indicated by the arrow in Illus. 18) will extend below the bottom of the fuselage by about ⅜″ or so.

Once you've folded both wings in exactly the same way, *Dart III* should look like the plane shown in Illus. 19.

Lift both wings so that they stick straight out from the fuselage. Turn *Dart III* so that the fuselage is down, and

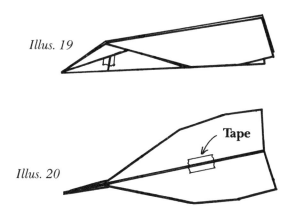

Illus. 19

Illus. 20

Tape

you're looking at the wings from above. Illus. 20 is this top view. Fasten the two wings together with a small piece of tape (like the one shown in Illus. 20).

Launch *Dart III* in the same manner that we used to launch *Darts I* and *II*. It will give you a long, steady flight. When *Dart III* loses power at the end of its flight, it should settle gently and smoothly to the ground.

Dart Junior

This little dart is only half the size of the three you've just constructed. Cut a sheet of notebook paper or typing paper in half, so that you have a piece of material 8½″ long by 5½″ wide.

Fold this half sheet of paper down the middle the long way. The folded paper should look like Illus. 21, which is exactly the same way the other *Darts* looked, only half their size.

Check the dotted line in Illus. 21 to see where you're now going to fold *Dart Junior*. Fold the side nearer to you, and then repeat the fold on the other side of the airplane. Begin this fold about 1″ from the upper left-hand corner of the paper.

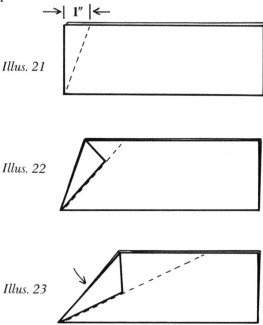

Illus. 21

Illus. 22

Illus. 23

With this fold in place, your airplane should look like the one shown in Illus. 22. The dotted line shown in this drawing indicates your next fold.

When you've folded both sides of *Dart Junior* (as called for in Illus. 22) your tiny dart should look like the one shown in Illus. 23.

When you fold along the dotted line shown in Illus. 23, the edge of the paper (indicated by the arrow) should come right down to the center fold, which is the bottom of the plane's fuselage. If the edge of the paper doesn't come quite to the center fold, or if the edge drops below the fold just a fraction of an inch, adjust the fold so that the paper's edge and the center fold are exactly even.

Once this fold is finished, you've reached Illus. 24. When you fold down the wing's edge along the dotted line shown in Illus. 24, make sure that the fold is parallel to the edge of the wing. Fold down about ⅜″ of the edge of the wing in this step.

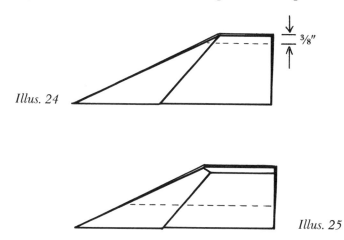

Illus. 24

⅜″

Illus. 25

For the final fold, check the dotted line shown in Illus. 25. Note that this new fold is exactly parallel to the original center fold (which has now become the bottom of the fuselage).

First fold the side nearer to you, and then repeat the fold on the airplane's other side. Crease the folds well and your aircraft should look like the one shown in Illus. 26

Illus. 26

Does my beak look like a fuselage? Don't answer that!

Unfold the wings so that they stick straight out from the fuselage, and then unfold the edges of the wings so that they come down from the wings at right angles. *Dart Junior* is now ready for a test flight.

Hold the plane between your thumb and your forefinger, about halfway between the nose and the tail, and launch it with a quick forward flip of your hand and arm. Two things should happen. First, *Dart Junior* should turn over in mid-flight and finish its flight upside down. Second, it will stall (it slows down and stops in midair) and come down nose-first in a fairly short distance.

To give *Dart Junior* a longer glide path slip a paper clip onto its fuselage, as shown in Illus. 27.

Illus. 27

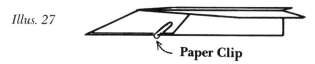

Paper Clip

Now take another test flight. *Dart Junior* should still turn over and fly upside down, but its flight should now be longer and smoother than it was before. Experiment with moving the paper clip closer to the nose and then nearer to the tail. When you find the exact spot where the paper clip allows *Dart Junior* to make its best flight, leave the clip there.

By moving the paper clip around you're "trimming" the airplane. When an airplane flies correctly, its said to be in perfect "trim."

Now you've folded four *Darts* in four different ways. Why not make some *Darts* of your own? For starters, try folding *Dart Junior* out of a full-size sheet of paper. Try folding *Darts I, II,* and *III* out of half-sheets of paper, and see how they fly.

Design your own *Darts.* Just remember to keep their noses heavy by making a number of folds which stack up layers of paper in the nose, and to keep the wingspread fairly narrow.

SHORT STUFF

2.
Short Stuff

Let's get acquainted with four paper airplanes we'll call "short stuff," because these flying machines end up being about half as long as the *Darts* you've just made. Because these paper airplanes are short and fairly wide, you'll see that they fly much differently from the *Darts*.

Stutter Step

You'll discover why this little airplane is called *Stutter Step* when you fly it.

Begin with a sheet of notebook paper or typing paper. Fold the sheet of paper in half the short way, so that it looks like the drawing shown in Illus. 28. Make sure that the folded edge of the paper is towards the left.

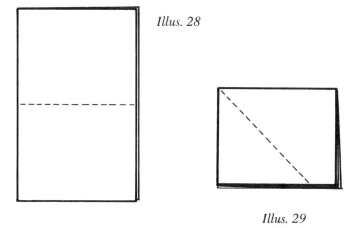

Illus. 28

Illus. 29

As you can see from the dotted line shown in Illus. 28, now fold the paper in half. Bring down the top edge towards the bottom when you make this fold.

With the fold in place, you've arrived at Illus. 29. Make absolutely certain that the fold you just made is at the top of the paper.

When you fold along the dotted line shown in Illus. 29, bring up the lower left-hand corner of the paper. Fold the top layer of paper, which is now two sheets thick. After you fold the top layer, repeat this fold on the other side of the airplane.

Check Illus. 30 to see how the finished fold looks. The edges of the paper you just folded should come right up to the folded edge of the paper. Now the bottom of *Stutter Step*'s fuselage is at the top of the paper you're folding.

Before you fold along the dotted line shown in Illus. 30, be sure that this fold is parallel to the bottom of the fuselage.

Begin by folding up the wing nearer to you along the dotted line. Crease this fold firmly into place. Repeat the

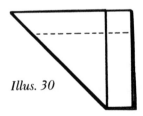

Illus. 30

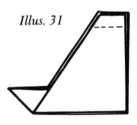

Illus. 31

process with the other wing. Once you've folded up both wings, your airplane should look much like the one shown in Illus. 31.

Be sure to make the fold shown in Illus. 31 so that it's parallel to the edge of the paper. Fold down the wing tip nearer to you and crease the fold, and then do the same for the other wing. Now the folding is finished. With these folds in place, you've arrived at Illus. 32.

Now unfold the wings, so that *Stutter Step* looks like the drawing shown in Illus. 33. Use two small strips of tape to tightly fasten together the sides of the fuselage. These tape strips can be seen in the drawing.

Once the sides of the fuselage are taped together, spread the airplane's wings so that they extend straight out at right angles from the fuselage. A top view of the project at this stage is shown in Illus. 34.

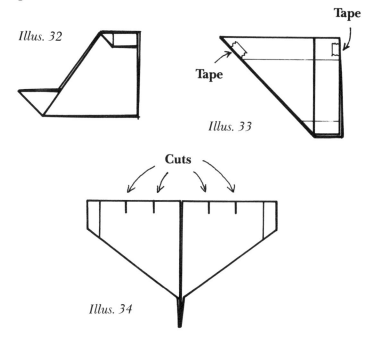

Illus. 32

Tape

Tape

Illus. 33

Cuts

Illus. 34

There are four cut lines (shown in Illus 34) at the rear, or "trailing" edge, of the plane's wings. Don't cut yet! When you make these scissor cuts, cut through only the *top* layer of material at the rear of the wings. Make the cuts ¼″ to ⅜″ long and a bit more than 1" apart on each wing. Now cut *only* the top layer of paper.

Once you've finished these cuts, bend the flap upwards between each pair of cuts to form control surfaces at the trailing edge of each wing. Bend these little flaps upwards, to give *Stutter Step* additional *lift*, to help keep it in the air.

Lift the wing tips upwards along their fold lines so that they stand straight up from the wings. Make sure that the wings are at right angles to the fuselage.

Launch *Stutter Step* by holding it at about the middle of the fuselage and by giving it a firm forward snap.

Don't be alarmed when your airplane flies a few feet and then stalls before falling to the ground; it just needs to be "trimmed" correctly.

When an airplane stalls, it's usually because it needs more weight in the nose in order to be in proper trim. Slip a paper clip onto the plane's nose. The drawing of *Stutter Step*'s nose, shown in Illus. 35, indicates how to do this.

Paper Clip ⟶    *Illus. 35*

Now test the plane again. If it still stalls, add a second paper clip and it should fly nicely. Try bending the two rear control flaps straight up, and then try them with the flaps only partway up. With just a little experimenting, you'll get the control flaps adjusted correctly. You can also try moving one paper clip a little bit towards the rear of the fuselage to see how that affects *Stutter Step*'s flight.

Now you'll see how this little airpline got its name, since it takes little stutters and steps during its flight.

Take a number of flights during which you change the position of the control flaps, and see what happens as you add paper clips or move one along the fuselage away from the nose. This is all a part of finding out exactly what combination of weight and flaps makes a certain paper airplane fly the way it does.

Tip: To make paper-airplane flying more fun, try bending up one control flap at a steeper angle than the other. This should cause your airplane to turn (or "bank") during flight.

If you want to experiment, go back to one of the *Darts* and try bending up the rear edge of one wing just a bit. This should cause the *Dart* to turn its nose upward. Just this tiny change will dramatically alter this plane's flight. Sometimes you can cause a *Dart* to turn over or spin as it flies if you bend up the rear of one wing and the rear of the other wing down.

Just remember that with all paper airplanes you can change the way they fly by bending upwards all (or part) of the wing's trailing edge.

Smoothie

Start with a sheet of notebook paper, typing paper, or computer paper, and fold it in half the short way. After folding the paper, make certain you place it on your table or desk so that the fold is to your left, as shown in Illus. 36. Fold down the top of the paper along the dotted line shown in Illus. 36.

Once this fold is in place, your paper will have a fold at the top and folds on the left just like the sheet seen in Illus. 37.

The dotted line shown in Illus. 37 indicates your next fold. When you make this fold, be sure to fold only the *top* section of *Smoothie* upwards. This section is two sheets thick, by the way.

Check Illus. 38 as you make this fold. The edge of the

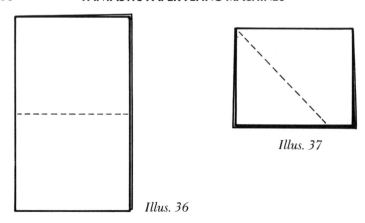

Illus. 37

Illus. 36

folded section comes right up to the fold at the top of the paper. The top of the paper will be the *bottom* of your fuselage.

Once you fold up the top layer into place, repeat the folding on the bottom layer; this will bring you to Illus. 38.

The dotted fold line shown in Illus. 38 is about 1″ from the top of the paper. Fold upwards the section of paper that's

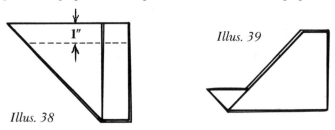

Illus. 39

Illus. 38

nearer to you along this dotted line. Crease the fold carefully. Make absolutely certain that this fold is parallel to the bottom of the fuselage. Fold upwards the lower section of paper in the same manner.

Congratulations! Here are your wings!

Watch the pin, OK?

Congratulations! You've just created wings for *Smoothie*. At this point, things should look very much like the drawing shown in Illus. 39.

Now that your airplane has wings, unfold them so your project looks like Illus. 40. Illus. 40 looks very much like Illus. 38.

Check the two pieces of tape shown in Illus. 40. Wrap a small piece of tape around the nose, as shown in the drawing, to help hold together the fuselage's sides tightly. Fold a

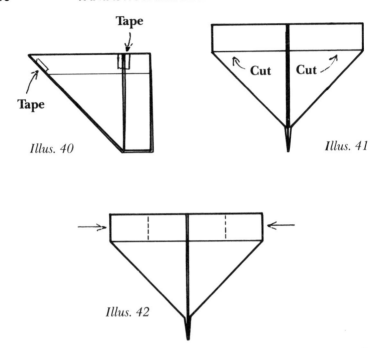

Illus. 40

Illus. 41

Illus. 42

second piece of tape around the fuselage, towards the rear of the airplane. This second piece of tape should hold the wing folds firmly in place.

Turn over *Smoothie* so that it looks like Illus. 41. It's time for a bit of careful cutting, but don't cut yet. You're going to make these cuts just a bit more than 1″ from the rear of your flying machine. Cut only the *top* layer of paper! This is *very* important. Carefully make the two cuts where indicated in Illus. 41. Once the cuts are finished, your paper airplane should look like Illus. 42.

When you fold the two tail sections along the dotted lines (shown in Illus. 42) you'll be folding only the top layer of paper which you just cut. Fold the two tail pieces in half, so that the edges indicated by the arrows in the drawing meet at the center of the fuselage.

With the folds in place, things should look much as they do in Illus. 43. Now fold the tail section into place, right at the

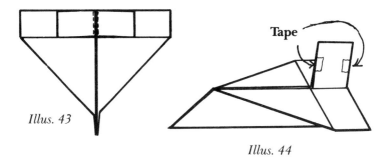

Illus. 43

Illus. 44

fuselage. The dotted lines in Illus. 43 indicate the fold you'll crease now.

Illus. 44 shows a side view of your finished *Smoothie*. Note the two strips of tape at the front and the rear of the upright tail section. The upright tail section is called a "vertical stabilizer." Wrap the two pieces of tape around the front ("leading" edge) and rear ("trailing" edge) of the vertical stabilizer.

Grasp *Smoothie* between your thumb and your forefinger, at about the middle of the fuselage, and launch it. Your *Smoothie* will probably stall. Your airplane's nose needs a bit of weight to trim it properly.

Slip a paper clip over *Smoothie*'s nose and launch it again. Most likely it won't fly perfectly. Do a little "trimming" and make your plane fly in a smooth glide path.

Begin by bending the trailing edges (the rear edges) of the wings just a bit. Don't fold them straight up. Instead, use your thumbs and forefingers to bend up or roll up the paper slightly. The arrows in Illus. 45 show where to do this bending or rolling.

Test fly your airplane again; it will probably stall again. When it does, add a *second* paper clip to its nose and launch it again.

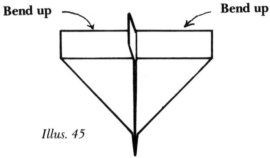

Bend up →   ← **Bend up**

Illus. 45

Now your *Smoothie* should fly in a way that matches its name. If your airplane doesn't fly smoothly, try some minor trim adjustments.

Try it with a bit more bend on the trailing edge of the wings. Then try the plane with less bend. Try moving one paper clip along the lower edge of the fuselage and back from the nose just a little way.

It should't take more than a few flights until you find the perfect combination of bend on the wings and the proper location for the paper clips, and then *Smoothie* will glide perfectly.

Tip: To help you successfully fold and fly paper airplanes, don't give up when one doesn't fly perfectly at first. Experiment with it. Add some weight to the nose when it stalls. Give it more lift by bending upwards the trailing edges of the wings. If your airplane is a total failure, just spend two minutes folding another.

Cruiser

All the fantastic paper flying machines you've folded so far were made with a rectangular sheet of paper. *Cruiser* is folded from a *square* piece of notebook paper or typing

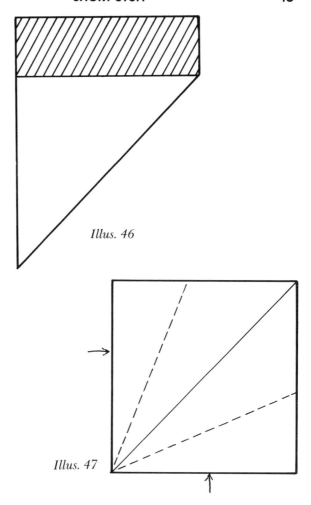

Illus. 46

Illus. 47

paper. Since notebook, typing, and computer paper all come as rectangles, first turn such a sheet of paper into a square; this will be simple.

Illus. 46 shows that the bottom right-hand corner of the paper has been folded up and over. The shaded portion of the paper shown in Illus. 46 should be cut off after the fold is made.

Unfold the paper and what you have left is a perfectly square sheet, as seen in Illus. 47. This square piece of paper has a diagonal fold line, which can also be seen in Illus. 47.

The two dotted lines in Illus. 47 show where to begin folding. When you make each fold, be sure that the edge of the material indicated by an arrow comes right to the center fold. When both folds are in place, the two edges will meet along the center fold and look exactly like Illus. 48.

The dotted line in Illus. 48 shows where to make your next fold. When this fold is in place, the pointed tip of material will come right up to the point at the opposite end of the paper, and your project should look just like Illus. 49.

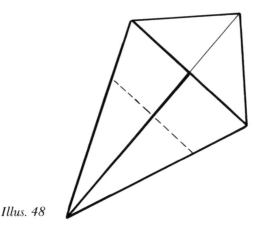

Illus. 48

When you make the fold shown by the dotted line in Illus. 49, fold only the *top* section of the paper (the one you just folded in the previous step). This fold should be 1″ from the lower edge of the airplane. Now your *Cruiser* can be seen in Illus. 50.

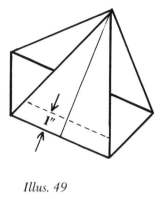

Illus. 49

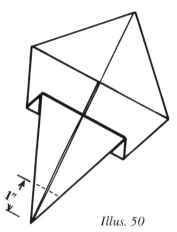

Illus. 50

The dotted line in Illus. 50 shows your next fold. Once, again, this fold is 1″ from the pointed end of the project.

With this fold in place, you're at Illus. 51. There's another dotted line in the drawing; this fold comes right at the little pointed tip of paper you just folded up into place.

Make the fold called for in Illus. 51, and you've reached the step pictured in Illus. 52.

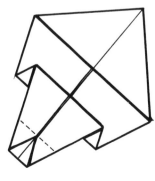

Illus. 51

Illus. 52

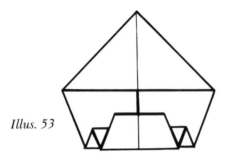

Illus. 53

There's a dotted fold line in Illus. 52. Once you finish that fold, *Cruiser* should look like the figure shown in Illus. 53.

Now fold your paper airplane along the original center fold. Once this is done, things should look like the drawing in Illus. 54. All those folded layers of material are hidden *inside* the airplane.

The dotted line in Illus. 54 will show you how to fold *Cruiser*'s wings into place. Notice that this fold line angles up very slightly from the nose towards the tail. This angle is important; don't make it too sharp.

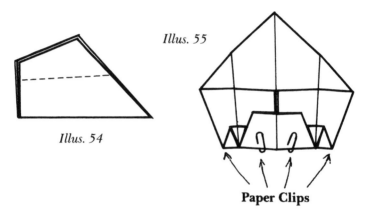

Illus. 55

Illus. 54

Paper Clips

Begin the fold at the nose at the point where the layers of folded paper are the thickest. Look ahead to Illus. 55, which is a top view showing *Cruiser* with its wings folded into place. See how the wing folds form that little triangle of material indicated by the arrows.

Fold the wing that's closer to you, and crease it carefully. Then fold the opposite wing in the same manner, and you've reached Illus. 55.

Slip a paper clip into each side of the nose, as shown in Illus. 55. Now test *Cruiser*. It should fly pretty well. However, you can make it fly even better with just a little bending.

Illus. 56 shows two arrows pointing to the trailing edges of *Cruiser*'s wings. Using your thumbs and forefingers to roll the paper upwards, bend these edges upwards just a bit. Don't bend straight up; a little upward roll works best.

Now test your airplane. It should cruise through the air with a dip or two as it glides along.

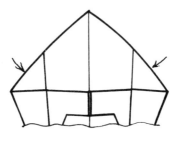

Illus. 56

Experiment with the trim until the airplane flies perfectly. Depending upon the weight of the paper you use, you may find that your *Cruiser* flies better with one paper clip right along the center fold rather than with the two shown in Illus. 55.

Little Beauty

The three *Short Stuff* paper airplanes you've already folded and flown are all great fliers, but *Little Beauty* may be the best of the bunch.

First fold a sheet of notebook paper, typing paper, or computer paper in half the long way. Unfold the paper and turn it over so that the fold you just put in place looks like a little mountain running the length of the paper. The paper should look like the sheet shown in Illus. 57.

The dotted lines in Illus. 57 show where to make the first folds. Make sure that the edges of the folded paper come

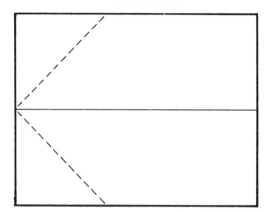

Illus. 57

right to the center fold. With these two folds in place, you've advanced to Illus. 58.

Check the dotted line shown in Illus. 58, and then make that fold. Once this fold is in place, your *Little Beauty* should look like the drawing in Illus. 59.

There are two dotted fold lines shown in the drawing. When you make the two folds called for in Illus. 59, be sure the edges of the folded paper meet right along the center fold.

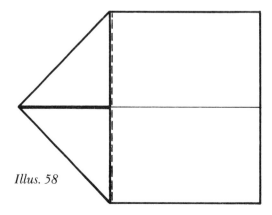

Illus. 58

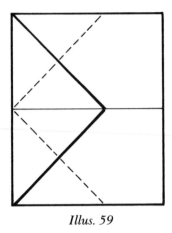

Illus. 59

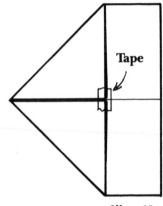

Illus. 60

With these two folds done correctly, your paper airplane is shown in Illus. 60. Illus. 60 shows a small piece of tape which will hold these folded pieces firmly in place from now on. Make certain that the tape overlaps the two corners of folded material and holds them fast to the fuselage.

Turn over *Little Beauty* so that it looks like the one shown in Illus. 61. Fold back the nose along the dotted line. Be very

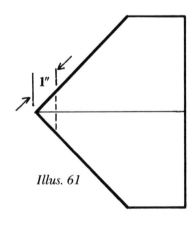

Illus. 61

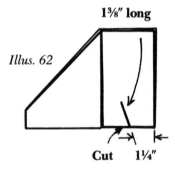

Illus. 62

careful making this nose. You're folding several layers of paper, but you're folding only 1″ of material.

Crease the fold firmly into place. Once you've done this folding, refold your paper airplane along the center fold, so that it looks like the drawing shown in Illus. 62.

Now make the cut indicated by the cut line shown in Illus. 62. Begin this cut 1¼″ from the rear of the fuselage. The cut angles towards the front of the airplane just a bit. The actual cut itself should be about 1⅜″ long. When making this scissor cut, hold the folded airplane firmly so that the layers of paper don't slip. It's important for this cut to be exactly the same on both sides of the fuselage.

With this bit of scissor work finished, you've reached Illus. 63. The dotted line in the drawing shows where to fold the end of the fuselage into a rear stabilizer. Fold both layers of paper towards you, so that your paper airplane looks like the one shown in Illus. 64. Now fold it back the other way, so that

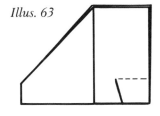

Illus. 63

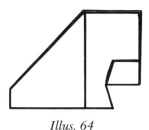

Illus. 64

it's hidden from sight. You're doing this folding so that the next step will be easier. After you've folded the stabilizer-to-be back and forth, fold it back so that it looks like the one shown in Illus. 65.

Spread the wings just a bit so that there's room for the stabilizer to fit between them. Then push up with your finger at the point shown by the arrow in Illus. 65. You're turning this much-folded area inside out. This little piece will fit right up inside the wings when you give it a poke and a push with your finger.

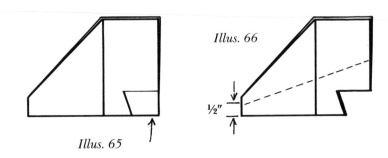

Illus. 66

½″

Illus. 65

With the stabilizer turned inside out, push the wings together firmly again and *Little Beauty* is shown in Illus. 66. The dotted line shown here is for your wing fold.

Study the fold before making it. See how it begins about ½″ above the bottom of the fuselage at the nose, and then angles up sharply towards the airplane's tail. Fold down the wing that's nearer to you, and crease the fold firmly. Be careful with this fold, because again you'll be folding several layers of paper at the nose.

If a tiny tear appears in one or more layers at the nose as you make this fold, don't worry about it. *Little Beauty* will still fly wonderfully well.

After folding the near wing, turn over the airplane and fold the second wing to match the first. Illus. 67 shows the plane after you've finished these wing folds.

Now open *Little Beauty*'s wings. The stabilizer will open as well. Illus. 68 shows a top view of *Little Beauty* ready to fly.

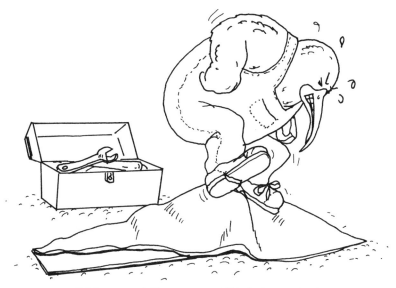

Fold, crease, fold, crease . . . This is frustrating!

Hold this great little airplane about halfway between the nose and the piece of tape, and launch it firmly. As your reward for careful folding, it will do an awesome job of flying.

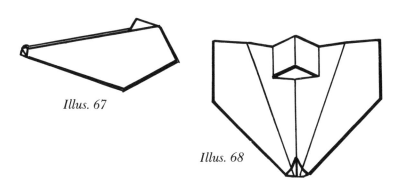

Illus. 67

Illus. 68

LONG-DISTANCE FLIERS

3.
Long-Distance Fliers

This chapter will show you how to fold four paper airplanes that specialize in long-distance flight.

Stealth

Once you've folded and taped *Stealth*, it will take off on a long, silent glide. When everything is working properly, *Stealth* will fly far enough to amaze you. In fact, it will sneak up on you! That's why *Stealth* is its name.

Start by folding a sheet of notebook paper or other paper in half the long way, so that the paper looks like the drawing shown in Illus. 69.

Next, fold on the dotted line shown in Illus. 69. Begin this fold about 2″ from the upper left-hand corner. Fold the top

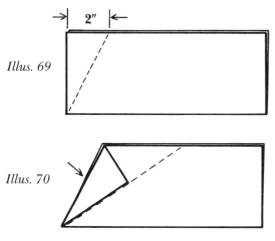

Illus. 69

Illus. 70

layer of paper *towards* you. After creasing the fold into place, fold the other side of the airplane so that it matches the first side.

With this first pair of folds in place, you've arrived at Illus. 70. The dotted line shows your next fold. When you make this fold, be sure that the edge of the paper (indicated by the arrow in the illustration) comes right down to the center fold. After folding the side nearer to you, turn over the plane and fold the second side so that it exactly matches your first fold. Once you've done this, *Stealth* is shown in Illus. 71.

Refold the center fold so that the triangular folded parts are now *inside* the airplane. *Stealth* should now look like the drawing shown in Illus. 72.

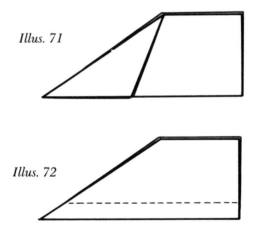

Illus. 71

Illus. 72

Check the dotted fold line shown in Illus. 72; note that it runs parallel to the center fold. Fold down both wings, one at a time, along this fold line. Be sure to crease these folds carefully. Your paper airplane has now reached the stage seen in Illus. 73.

Lift the airplane's wings upwards, so that your project looks like the drawing shown in Illus. 74. *Stealth* now looks the same as it did in Illus. 72, except that the dotted fold line

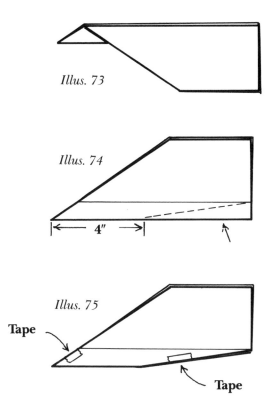

Illus. 73

Illus. 74

|← 4″ →|

Illus. 75

Tape

Tape

has now become a folded line. In Illus. 74, the dotted line indicates your next fold. Be very careful making this fold; it begins about 4″ in back of the nose point. See how this fold runs upwards to meet the wing fold you just made.

Fold both layers of paper towards you along the dotted line shown in Illus. 74 and crease the fold. Now fold back both layers in the opposite direction and crease that fold. This folding and creasing will make the next step easier.

Once you've folded and creased the fold in both directions, push up on the center fold, at the point shown by the arrow in Illus. 74. You'll probably have to use both hands to turn this long, narrow triangle of paper inside out. Once you've turned it inside out, the long, narrow triangle will be inside *Stealth*. From the side, your project looks just like Illus. 75.

Check the two strips of tape shown in Illus. 75. Put them in place now, so that they hold the sides of *Stealth*'s fuselage tightly together.

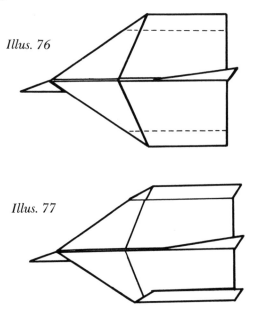

Illus. 76

Illus. 77

Illus. 76 shows a top view of your nearly finished paper airplane. Fold up the edges of both wings along the dotted lines shown in Illus. 76. Illus. 77 shows *Stealth* with its wing edges folded up into place.

Now give *Stealth* a test flight if you wish; it will probably stall. Add a paper clip to the airplane's nose and fly it again.

Stealth should take off and fly like a dream on a long, smooth glide path. You may want to try moving the paper clip rearwards a bit to check the trim, but this awesome paper airplane should fly perfectly without any need to work on its trim.

Arrow

Here's another *Dart* which is a fantastic long-distance flier.

Since this is a *Dart*, fold your paper in half the long way. Illus. 78 shows the folded paper complete with a dotted line indicating where to make your next fold.

Begin this fold about 2″ from the upper left-hand corner of your paper. Fold the nearer wing first, and then turn over the paper and fold the other wing to match the first. When this is done, you've moved on to Illus. 79.

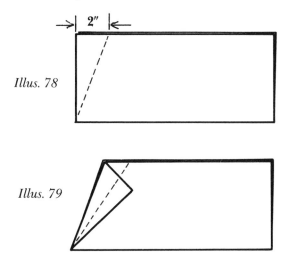

Illus. 78

Illus. 79

Illus. 79 shows another dotted line. Fold the triangle of paper from your first fold exactly in half. Once you've done this folding for both sides of the airplane, *Arrow* should look pretty much like the drawing shown in Illus. 80.

Fold along the dotted line shown in Illus. 80; simply fold along the edge of the fold you just finished. Make this fold, one wing at a time.

This brings *Arrow* to the stage shown in Illus. 81. There's another dotted fold line shown in the drawing. Once again, this new fold follows the edge of the fold you've just completed. Simply fold over the wing's edges, one side at a time, crease the folds, and glance ahead to Illus. 82.

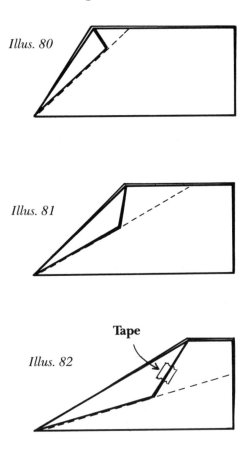

Illus. 80

Illus. 81

Tape

Illus. 82

With all this folding finished, things should look just like the drawing in Illus. 82. A small piece of tape will help hold all these wing folds where they belong. Put this tape onto *Arrow* now, and do the same for the second wing (which can't be seen in the drawing).

Now that you've applied two little chunks of tape to hold those wing folds in place, it's time for one more folding task. As you can see by the dotted line shown in Illus. 82, this fold is also going to run right along the edge of all those layers of folded paper you've been stacking on top of one another.

Make this fold in both wings, making totally certain that the two wings match exactly. When this is done, *Arrow* should look just like the drawing shown in Illus. 83.

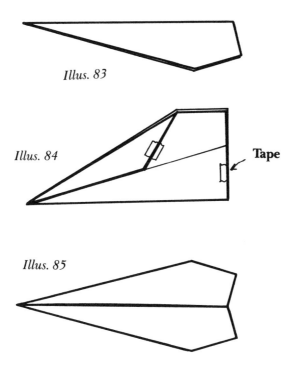

Illus. 83

Illus. 84   **Tape**

Illus. 85

The tape goes on the plane, not us!

Crease the wing folds well so *Arrow's* wings will stay in place. Now lift up the wings again so that your paper airplane looks like the one shown in Illus. 84.

As you can see in Illus. 84, it's time for one final bit of taping. Wrap a little chunk of tape around the rear of the fuselage to hold both sides of it tightly together. Make certain that the top edge of this tape comes almost to the fold, as can be seen in the drawing.

With this taping finished, and when viewed from the top, your completed *Arrow* should look just like Illus. 85.

Arrow should fly perfectly without any need to adjust the trim in any way. This is a good paper airplane for steady long-distance flights.

If you wish, experiment to see what happens when you bend up the wings' trailing edges just a bit. Try bending one up and leaving the other alone, or try bending one trailing edge up and the other down.

Tip: Experiment with *Arrow*'s wing trailing edges to increase *drag*, or air resistance. These changes will slow *Arrow* down and cause it to fly a shorter distance. To overcome this added drag, slip a paper clip onto the airplane's nose and see how this affects the plane's trim.

Free Spirit

Before you begin to cut and fold, there's one thing you need to know: This paper flying machine is for *outdoor* flying only. *Free Spirit* is for the outdoors, or for the school gym (if you're allowed to fly paper airplanes in the gym).

Begin by cutting a piece of paper file folder 9″ by 11″. You'll use most of one side of a standard manila file folder.

Fold the piece of material in half the short way, so that you have a doubled piece of file folder 9″ high and 5½″ wide. Crease this fold firmly. Since file folder material is fairly stiff, pay careful attention to creasing this fold and the next ones.

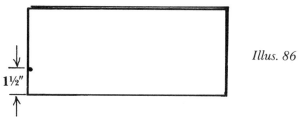

1½″

Illus. 86

One way to crease a fold in heavy material is to use the handle of an ordinary table knife. Hold the knife firmly in your hand and press down hard on the handle as you run it along the fold you want to crease. Illus. 86 shows the folded piece of file folder.

Illus. 86 shows a dot at the left-hand side of the material. This dot is exactly 1½″ above the fold. Use a ruler to draw a line from this dot to the corner of the wing at the upper right-hand corner of the material.

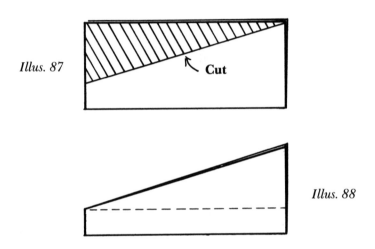

Illus. 87

Cut

Illus. 88

This line has been drawn in Illus. 87. Once you've drawn this line, use a pair of sharp scissors to cut along the line; this will remove a triangular piece of the material (shaded in the drawing). Hold both sides of the folded material firmly together so that the bottom one doesn't slip. Cut both wings at the same time, so that they're exactly alike when you finish. Illus. 88 shows how things will look after you've finished cutting.

Check the dotted line, which indicates your next fold. This fold line is parallel to the center fold and is 1½″ above the center fold.

Fold down the near wing and crease the fold, as you did for the center fold. Turn over *Free Spirit* and fold the second wing into place. Crease this fold well. At this stage, your airplane should look like the one shown in Illus. 89.

Lift up the wings so that your airplane looks like Illus. 90. This drawing looks much like Illus. 88, doesn't it?

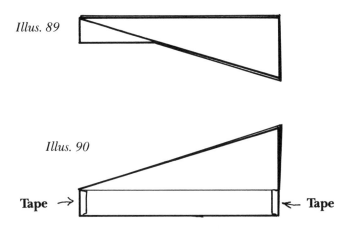

Illus. 89

Illus. 90

Tape →   ←— **Tape**

Note the tape at the nose and the tail. Put these two pieces of tape in place now. Make sure that both sides of the fuselage come together before you press the tape onto the airplane.

Now cut a chunk of material from a cereal box. This piece should be 1¼″ by 3″. The dotted line in Illus. 91 shows where you're going to fold this little strip of material in half. Crease this fold just as you did the file-folder folds.

Now slip the folded piece of cereal-box cardboard over *Free Spirit*'s nose and tape it into place, as shown in Illus. 92.

Wrap one strip of tape around the bottom edge of this nose piece and a second strip of tape around the end of the cardboard. You could use two shorter strips of tape for the

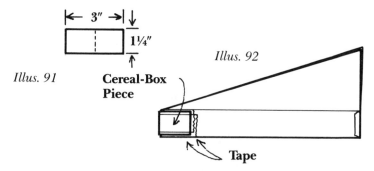

Illus. 91

Cereal-Box Piece

Illus. 92

Tape

end of the cardboard instead of wrapping one longer strip around both sides of the fuselage.

Illus. 93 shows a top view of *Free Spirit*. Do a little *bending* (not folding, but *bending*), of the trailing edges of the airplane's wings. Carefully bend or roll the trailing edges upwards. At the wing tips (shown by the single arrows in Illus. 93), try to bend or roll upwards about ¼″ of the material. As you work towards the fuselage, bend up less material. By the time you get to the points indicated by the double arrows, you want to have only about ⅛″ of material bent upwards.

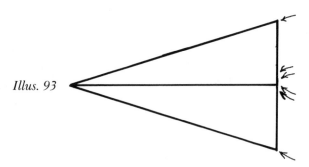

Illus. 93

Take your time doing this. Try to keep the bent (or rolled) trailing edges smooth. What you want is to have ¼″ of material at the wingtips, and half that amount rolled upwards by the time you get to the fuselage.

Your first test flight will probably be disappointing, because *Free Spirit*'s trim is only partly finished. You can do your first test in the living room, if you wish. Later it will be time to move outside or to the school gym.

Free Spirit will probably stall and flutter, because you'll need to work on its trim. Begin by slipping a large paper clip over the nose. If you have one of those super-size paper clips, use it.

Once you start to use paper clips to help trim this paper airplane, it's time to test-fly it outdoors, because eventually you're going to get *Free Spirit* trimmed just right. When that happens, the plane will take off and really glide. This paper airplane is much heavier than the ones you've been folding from notebook paper or typing paper. It may knock over breakable objects in the house, and it can even chip the paint from the living room wall!

Try flying *Free Spirit into* any breeze and *with* the breeze.

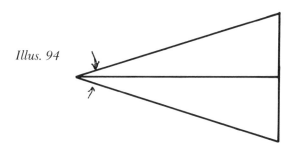

Illus. 94

Illus. 94 shows a top view of this airplane. Notice the pair of arrows near the airplane's nose. Very carefully bend down the first 3″ of material from the nose back along the side of the wing. Make these bends very gentle. Bend about ¼″ of the leading edge of each wing, but make this bend very slight.

The side view in Illus. 95 shows that these wing bends only depress the edges of the material a very little bit. By doing this bending, you'll be increasing *Free Spirit*'s lift.

Test-fly *Free Spirit* again. Add another big paper clip or a couple of small ones, as necessary.

Experiment by lowering or raising the bent or folded control flaps on the trailing edges of the wings.

Once you have this great airplane trimmed properly, it will fly in a smooth path for as much as 50′. That's another reason why *Free Spirit* is an outdoor airplane.

Illus. 95

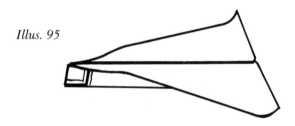

Gemini

Gemini is the astrological sign for the twins. You'll need *two* sheets of notebook paper or computer paper or typing paper to construct *Gemini*.

First fold one sheet of paper in half the short way. Illus. 96 shows this sheet with its fold already in place.

Illus. 96

½″

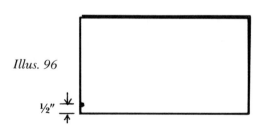

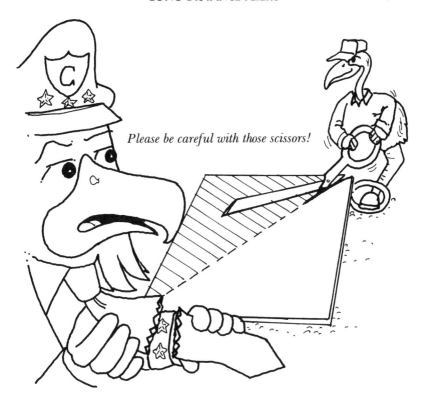

Please be careful with those scissors!

Illus. 96 also shows a dot, located ½″ up from the bottom fold on the left-hand side of the material. Measure for that dot and put it in place now.

In Illus. 97, draw a line from the dot you just marked to the upper right-hand corner of the paper.

After you draw the line called for in Illus. 97, hold both sides of the paper firmly together and cut along the line, discarding the shaded area in the drawing. Don't let the bottom sheet of paper slip, or your *Gemini* will be lopsided.

Illus. 98 shows what your airplane looks like after you've done that careful bit of cutting.

There's also a dotted fold line shown in Illus. 98. Study this line for just a second before starting to fold. This fold line starts at the very bottom edge of the airplane's wing on the left, and angles up so that it finishes exactly 2″ from the bottom of the material at the right.

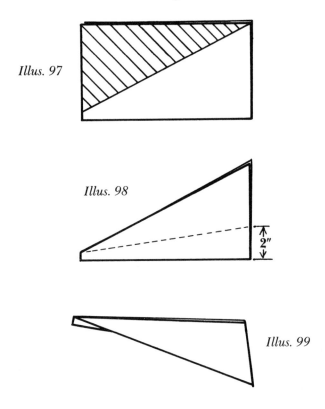

Illus. 97

Illus. 98

2″

Illus. 99

Fold down the wing nearer to you, and crease the fold. Repeat the process with the second wing. Once you've folded both wings, *Gemini* should look like the drawing shown in Illus. 99.

Set aside this piece of material for the time being. Now it's time to deal with the other part of *Gemini*.

Begin by folding the second sheet of paper in half the long way, and then unfold it, so that it looks just like Illus. 100.

The dotted line in Illus. 100 shows where to make your next fold. Make sure this fold begins exactly in the lower left-hand corner of the material and angles up to the center fold. Fold this crease carefully and you've arrived at Illus. 101.

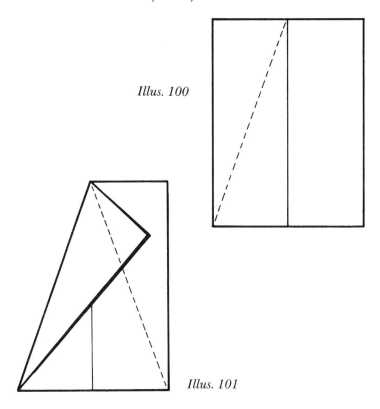

Illus. 100

Illus. 101

Carefully examine the dotted fold line shown in Illus. 101. You're going to make exactly the same fold on the right side of the center fold as you just made on the left side. Simply begin this second fold at the lower right-hand side of the material and make sure it goes right to the center fold.

Once this fold is in place, you've formed the nose point for this half of *Gemini*. You also have a flap of leftover material sticking out, as seen in Illus. 102. The arrow in the drawing indicates this flap.

Fold this flap around the other side of the airplane, as indicated by the dotted line. When you turn over the airplane, the opposite side is shown in Illus. 103. Use a bit of tape to firmly fasten down the flap you just folded around the airplane.

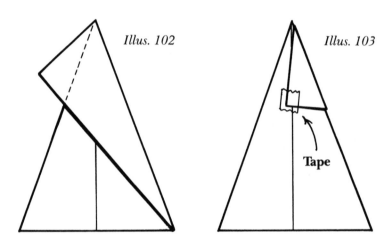

Illus. 102

Illus. 103

Tape

Turn over the airplane again, so that it looks like the one shown in Illus. 104.

Now it's time to join *Gemini*'s two halves. Leave the part you've just been working on so that it lies flat on the table or desk, as shown in Illus. 104.

Place the part of this fantastic flying machine you made first on top of the one lying on the table. The flat side of the original piece of airplane fits against the second piece of *Gemini*; *Gemini*'s fuselage now sticks straight up, as shown in

Illus. 105. As you can see in Illus. 105, it's time for some tape, once again.

Make certain that the two sides of the fuselage (the long slender triangle of paper sticking up from the airplane) come together so that there's no space between the two sides. Make sure that the center folds of both parts of the airplane are directly in line with one another.

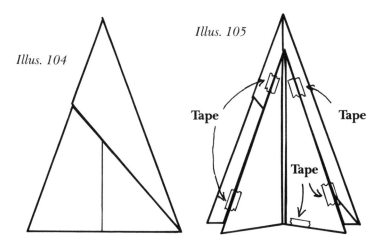

Illus. 104

Illus. 105

As you can see in Illus. 105, there's about 2″ of space between the nose point on the bottom section and the nose point on the upper section. The points of the tail section of the top section stick out just a bit behind the other section.

Once you have the two parts of *Gemini* lined up perfectly, tape the two sections together with two strips of tape along each side of the top section.

When you get to the fifth (and final) piece of tape at the tail, apply this little chunk of tape so that it holds the two tail sections together. *This is important.* Without this little bit of tape, *Gemini* will vibrate in flight, and it won't fly as well as it does with the tape in place.

Turn over *Gemini* so that it looks like the figure seen in Illus. 106.

There are two little fold lines shown in Illus. 106. Fold down the corners of only the top section of *Gemini* along these fold lines.

These folds begin right at the edge of the wingtips of the bottom (or fuselage) half of *Gemini*. Each fold is about 2″ long. Fold down the wingtips along each dotted line.

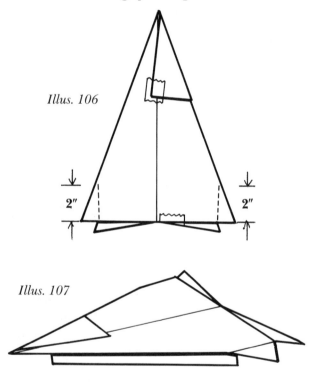

Illus. 106

2″   2″

Illus. 107

Illus. 107 shows a side view of *Gemini* ready to fly. Grasp the fuselage about halfway back from the nose and give the plane a firm, steady launch. If *Gemini* wants to turn upward, just slip a paper clip onto its nose and try it again.

Gemini is an awesome flier, and it's probably much different from any airplane any of your friends have folded and flown. It will give you a steady glide path, and it flies for a long distance.

Take *Gemini* outdoors, and it will cover 50′ in a single flight.

EXPERIMENTAL FLYING MACHINES

4.
Experimental Flying Machines

In this chapter you'll learn how to build four paper flying machines which look and fly differently from those you folded in the first three chapters.

Once you've discovered that these paper airplanes (which don't look a whole lot like the sort of airplanes you're used to seeing) can do a great job of flying, you'll probably want to design some experimental flying machines of your own.

Slider

You'll need a sheet of notebook paper or typing paper for *Slider*, but your first step *isn't* to fold the paper in half. Begin by cutting off 2″ from the long side of the paper. This leaves you with a sheet of material about 6½″ wide and 11″ long.

Now that you've cut the paper to size, fold it in half the short way. After making this fold, unfold the paper so that it looks like the paper shown in Illus. 108.

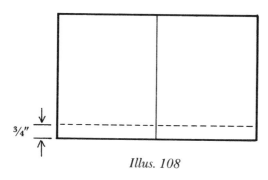

Illus. 108

The dotted fold line shown in Illus. 108 is exactly ¾″ from the edge of the paper. Fold over that ¾″-wide strip and crease the fold. Once you've made the fold called for in Illus. 108, *Slider* should look like Illus. 109.

When you make the fold along the dotted line shown in Illus. 109, just fold over the ¾″-strip once again. Once you've

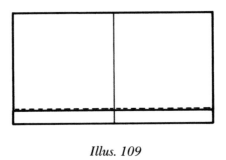

Illus. 109

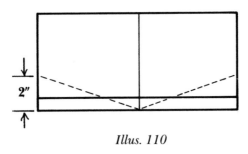

Illus. 110

done this, you should have three layers of paper at *Slider*'s nose, and you've also reached Illus. 110.

The pair of dotted lines shown in Illus. 110 indicates two folds; each begins at the center fold and angles back onto *Slider*'s wings. Make each fold so that it starts at the center of the aircraft and ends up exactly 2″ back from the leading edge of the wing. Check ahead to Illus. 111 to see how things look once these folds are in place; now make the folds.

Illus. 111

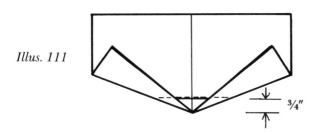

3/4″

The fold called for in Illus. 111 is (once again) ¾″ from the airplane's nose. Once again, just fold over those layers of

paper you've already folded into place. Be careful making this fold, since you're dealing with several layers of paper, and the fold itself is fairly short. Crease the fold firmly.

Now you've reached Illus. 112, where you'll see another dotted line in the drawing.

Again, crease the finished fold well, so that *Slider*'s nose (which is also the leading edge of its wing) will stay in place.

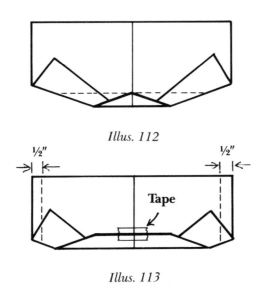

Illus. 112

Illus. 113

With this fold in place, you've arrived at Illus. 113. Examine the piece of tape shown in the drawing. Press a 2"-strip of tape firmly into place to make certain *Slider* doesn't come undone.

Illus. 113 also shows a pair of dotted lines where you'll make your final folds. Fold down ½" of material at each end of *Slider*'s wings. Crease these folds and make sure the wingtips now point straight down at right angles to the rest of the wing. In Illus. 114 you can see *Slider* ready to fly.

Slip a paper clip onto the leading edge of *Slider*'s nose, right on the center fold. This airplane will need the paper clip for proper trim. Be sure that the small part of the paper clip is on *top* of the wing. This is important!

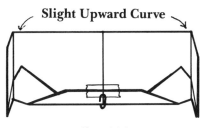

Slight Upward Curve

Illus. 114

Take a close look at the trailing edges of *Slider*'s wings (or does *Slider* have just one wing?). You'll notice that the rear wing edges are curved slightly upwards between the center fold and each wingtip. This is due to the way *Slider* is folded. These slight curves in the airplane's wings help give it a bit of extra lift.

To launch *Slider*, hold it by the trailing edge of the wing (or is it *wings*?) with your forefinger on *top* of the wing, and your thumb and middle finger *beneath* the wing.

Don't snap *Slider* to get it flying. Just hold it as high as you can and gently push the airplane into flight. If things are perfect, *Slider* will sail off in a nice, gentle downward glide clear across the room. If the airplane goes nose-down for a short, crashing flight, there are two possible problems.

First, try flying the airplane in the opposite direction from which you just tested it. Because *Slider* is nothing more than a slightly curved wing, it reacts to even the slightest draft or breeze. *Slider* won't tolerate air currents without having them affect the way it flies (or doesn't fly).

If you try flying *Slider* in several directions and it still noses down sharply, remove the paper clip and put on a smaller clip.

Slider is completely different from any other paper airplane you've flown before. Find a calm room in which to fly it, and it will amaze anyone who sees *Slider* and thinks that a flying machine which is just a wing can't fly.

T-Bird

T-bird was an experimental airplane when my wife and her friends flew it in their eighth-grade class about forty years ago.

First fold a sheet of notebook paper, typing paper, or computer paper in half the long way. Leave it folded, so that it looks like the drawing shown in Illus. 115.

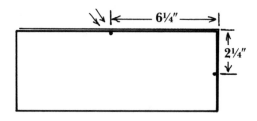

Illus. 115

Measure down 2¼″ from the upper right-hand corner of the folded paper, and make the dot indicated by the single arrow in Illus. 115.

Next, measure over 6¼″ from the same upper right-hand corner and make the dot indicated by the double arrows in the drawing. Now draw a line 2¼″ straight down from the second dot (the one shown by double arrows).

Connect the end of that line with the first dot you drew. The first dot is the one to which the single arrow points. Illus. 116 shows these two lines drawn in.

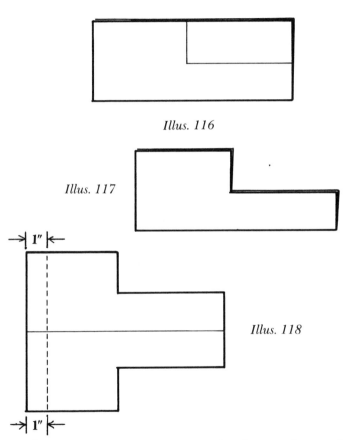

Illus. 116

Illus. 117

Illus. 118

Hold the two layers of paper firmly together, and with your scissors cut along the two lines you just drew. Don't let the bottom layer of paper slip as you're cutting. When you finish cutting, *T-Bird* should look like Illus. 117. Unfold the paper and things should look like Illus. 118.

Illus. 118 shows the first of many fold lines. Fold along the dotted line; make this fold just a bit less than 1″ from the edge of the paper. With this first fold in place, you've reached Illus. 119.

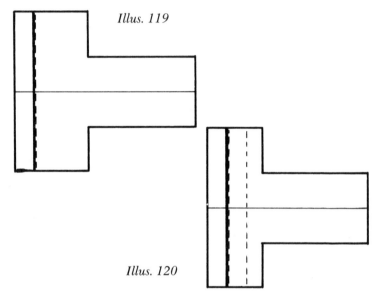

Illus. 119

Illus. 120

When you make the next fold, as indicated by the dotted line shown in Illus. 119, simply fold over the double layer you created by your first fold. Once this fold is completed, you've reached Illus. 120.

Note that there are two dotted fold lines shown in Illus. 120. They indicate you're going to fold over the triple layer for the first fold and then fold it over again for the second fold. When you finish the final fold, you'll notice that the folded edge probably sticks out past the edge of the paper where you cut a few minutes ago; this is just fine. Now you've arrived at Illus. 121.

Refold *T-Bird* along its center fold and things should look like Illus. 122.

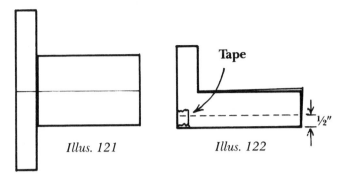

Illus. 121   *Illus. 122*

Illus. 122 shows a dotted fold line as well as a piece of tape. The fold is parallel to the center fold, which in turn is the bottom of *T-Bird*'s fuselage. This fold is ½" above the center fold. Note that the tape comes to this fold line but doesn't extend above it.

Wrap a ½"-piece of tape around the front of the fuselage now. This tape will hold together the front of *T-Bird*'s nose during flight. Once the tape is in place, fold down the side nearer to you along the dotted fold line. Crease the fold. Turn over *T-Bird* and make a similar fold on the opposite side of the aircraft.

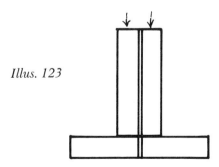

Illus. 123

Illus. 123 is a top view of *T-Bird* all folded and ready for flight. As you can see, *T-Bird*'s fuselage has now become a pair of wings with that last fold. The "wings" at the front of *T-Bird* make a horizontal stabilizer.

Slip a paper clip over the piece of tape on *T-Bird*'s nose and launch the plane with a steady forward flip of your hand and arm.

If *T-Bird*'s nose dips down in flight, bend or roll the trailing edges of its wings upwards a bit. The arrows in Illus. 123 show where to bend.

Should *T-Bird* nose upwards during flight, bend those trailing wing edges down just a bit.

Trim *T-Bird* by adjusting the trailing edges of its wings. Surprise people by showing them that this strange-looking airplane really does fly!

X-1

The "X" in *X-1*'s name stands for *experimental*. When you build and fly *X-1* you'll agree that it certainly looks experimental. *X-1* is different from any other paper flying machine you've made so far.

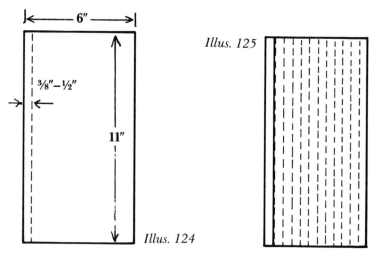

Illus. 125

Illus. 124

First trim a strip of paper from the side of a sheet of notebook paper or typing paper, so that you end up with a sheet of material 6″ wide and 11″ long. This sheet of paper can be seen in Illus. 124.

The drawing shows a fold line. This fold should be from ⅜″ to ½″ from the edge of the paper. Make this fold now.

In Illus. 125, the first fold is in place. Also in the drawing you can see a whole series of fold lines. To make these folds just begin folding the first folded strip over and over. Crease each fold as you make it. Try to make each fold right at the edge of the layers of paper, which will begin to build up as you fold the paper over and over.

When you've finished all this over-and-over folding, you'll have a strip of material 11″ long and ½″ or so wide and many, many layers thick. It should look just like Illus. 126.

You're going to turn this stack of paper layers into a fuselage for your *X-1*. Begin unfolding the sheet of material

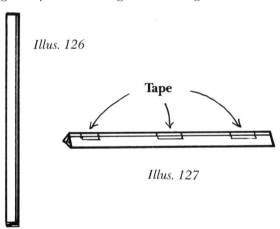

Illus. 126

Illus. 127

so that it looks like it did to begin with, except that it now has many folds in it.

Refold the paper so that it forms a long, skinny triangular piece which looks like the one shown in Ilus. 127. Form the triangle with the first three layers of paper, and then just continue to fold the paper around the triangle.

When you finish, use three small pieces of tape (like the ones shown in Illus. 127) to hold things together. With this folding and taping finished, set the fuselage aside for the time being.

Next, cut a piece of material 3″ wide and 4½″ long. This chunk of paper is shown in Illus. 128.

The dotted line in Illus. 128 shows where to make your first fold. This fold should be ¾″ from the edge of the paper.

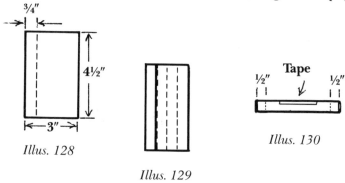

Illus. 128

Illus. 129

Illus. 130

Once this fold is made, you've come to the step shown by Illus. 129. As you can see, you'll be making three more folds in the same way you folded the fuselage. Just fold the double layer of paper over and over and over again. Crease each fold as you make it. Once you've made all these folds, you've come to Illus. 130.

Leave the folded material just the way it is. A strip of tape has been folded around the loose flap of paper to keep this part of *X-1* from unfolding in flight.

After you put the tape in place, fold up the ends of this piece of material. The two dotted fold lines shown in Illus. 130 are ½″ from either end of the material. Fold up these ends now and crease the folds, so that the ends stand straight up at right angles to the main part of the material.

The piece you just taped and folded will be the horizontal stabilizer for your *X-1*, by the way. You'll attach this piece near the front of the fuselage in just a minute or so.

Now cut a sheet of paper 8½" by a bit less than 7". Just cut off a little less than 7" from the end of a sheet of computer paper or typing paper and you've got it. This sheet of material, along with its first fold line, is shown in Illus. 131.

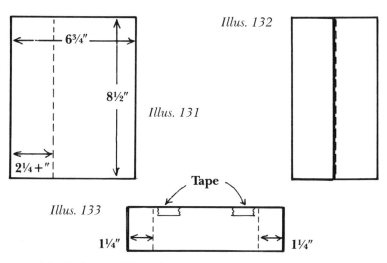

Illus. 132

Illus. 131

Illus. 133

This fold should be a fraction more than 2¼" from the left-hand side of the paper.

Once you've made the first fold, you've arrived at Illus. 132. There's just one dotted fold line in this drawing. Simply fold over the double layer you created a second ago.

Illus. 133 shows how to create the main wing for the *X-1* in just about the same way you folded and taped the horizontal stabilizer.

To hold the wing together, use two short strips of tape to wrap around the loose layer of paper.

Where's the top?

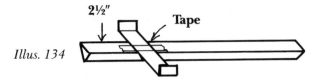

Where's the top?

Now fold up the wingtips, as shown by the pair of dotted lines. Make these folds about 1¼″ from the ends of the wings.

After all this cutting, folding, and taping, it's time to put X-1 together.

Begin with the fuselage and horizontal stabilizer. As you can see in Illus. 134, tape the stabilizer onto the top of the

2½″   **Tape**

Illus. 134

fuselage. Which side's the top? Whichever side you choose; they're both the same.

Place the stabilizer on top of the fuselage exactly 2½″ from the nose of *X-1*. Turn the stabilizer so that the tape you put on to hold it together is towards the rear of the airplane. To be sure that the airplane is evenly balanced, make certain you have the same amount of stabilizer on the right side of the fuselage as you do on the left.

Now attach the stabilizer to the fuselage, using a strip of tape which goes over the top of the horizontal stabilizer and extends about 1″ farther towards the nose and tail of the airplane.

Add the main wing in exactly the same way you just attached the horizontal stabilizer. Illus. 135 shows that the

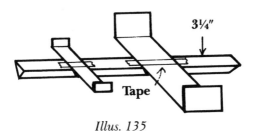

Illus. 135

taped side of the main wing is towards the rear of the airplane. Locate the rear edge of the main wing about 3¼″ from the tail end of the fuselage. Once again, make certain you keep your plane in balance. There must be as much wing to the right of the fuselage as there is to the left side.

Run a strip of tape over the top of the wing and onto the top of the fuselage. The tape should extend past the wing's leading and trailing edges about 2″.

Slip a paper clip onto the top side of *X-1*'s nose and give the plane a test flight. The best way to launch this paper airplane is to hold the fuselage between your thumb and your middle finger, with the tip of your index finger pushing against the rear end of the fuselage. Launch *X-1* as if you were throwing a dart. Remember that the main wing is at the rear of the airplane. Launch the plane with the smaller horizontal stabilizer facing forward.

If you decide you need two paper clips at the nose, slip one clip onto each of the two lower sides of the fuselage. One clip goes on top. Two go onto the bottom sides to keep *X-1* in balance. One clip on top is all you should need for this model.

After you've flown *X-1* a time or two, turn it over and launch it upside down. It will surprise you by flying perfectly, and then, near the end of its flight, it will roll over, so that it lands with its fuselage down!

Since "X" stands for *experimental*, don't be afraid to experiment. Build an *X-2* with a smaller main wing. See how your airplane flies if you tape the stabilizer and wing nearer to one another or nearer to the ends of the fuselage.

If an experimental model crashes, change the wing position or size and try again. Making new kinds of airplanes is what building and flying paper airplanes is all about.

Needle

Most of the fantastic paper flying machines you've folded have been made from a full sheet of notebook paper. Let's see what you can do using an 8½"-square sheet of paper.

If you've forgotten how to turn a rectangular sheet of paper into a square, turn back to page 43 now.

Once you've folded the paper and cut off the extra flap of material, unfold the sheet so it looks like Illus. 136.

When you make the two folds called for by the pair of dotted lines shown in Illus. 136, make sure that the edges of the paper come right to the center fold. Study how the paper

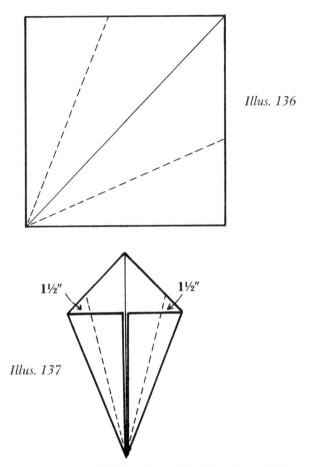

Illus. 136

Illus. 137

1½″   1½″

edges meet at the center fold in Illus. 137 after these folds are made.

With this pair of folds in place, and with your *Needle* looking like the figure in Illus. 137, make the next pair of folds, which are shown as dotted lines in the drawing.

Before you begin folding, study Illus. 137. See how these folds begin right at *Needle*'s nose point and run towards the trailing edges of the wings at an angle. It's a good idea to measure along the wings' trailing edges exactly 1½″ from the corner of the material and to put a dot there before you make the folds.

Illus. 137 shows these dots, which will help you to make the folds in exactly the proper places.

Once you've folded over the wing edges along the dotted lines in Illus. 137, *Needle* should look just like the figure shown in Illus. 138.

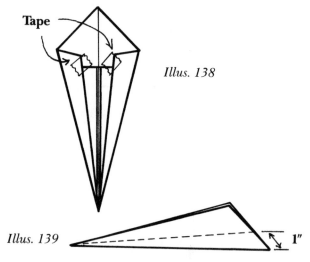

Tape

Illus. 138

Illus. 139   1″

Now stick on two little chunks of tape to help hold things together as you finish your folding, and then when you fly *Needle*. Study Illus. 138 to see how these tape chunks fasten down the paper you just folded so that these flaps of material are stuck fast to the fuselage. Notice also the corners of the first folding are covered by part of the tape.

Once the tape pieces are in place, refold *Needle* along the original center fold. The tape and all those folded flaps will now vanish inside the folded airplane, a drawing of which appears in Illus. 139.

Don't start just yet to fold along the dotted line shown in Illus. 139. Read how to do it first, and this final folding will be simple.

As you can see in the drawing, this fold begins at the airplane's nose and angles upwards towards the tail. This fold follows the edge of the wing flap you just taped into place; this flap is now hidden from view.

Deal with the wing that's nearer to you. Be extremely careful when you start this fold because it takes just a bit of care at the nose (which is long and like a needle).

To make this fold properly, pull the top wing towards you. Make the fold right along the edge of the wing flap. The finished fold will end up 1″ (or just a fraction more) from the tail point. This measurement is shown in Illus. 139, and it's there so you can check yourself to be sure your fold is going in the proper direction.

Once you've folded the near wing and creased it, turn over *Needle* and fold the second wing so that it matches the first. With these final folds in place, *Needle* should look like the figure shown in Illus. 140.

Illus. 140

Spread *Needle*'s wings so that they stick out at right angles to the fuselage. The airplane, ready to fly, looks like Illus. 141 when seen from the top.

Hold the fuselage between your thumb and your fore-finger about two-thirds of the way back from the nose. Point the airplane's nose slightly upwards and launch it firmly, but not *too* hard.

Near the end of *Needle*'s flight, when it's losing power, it will probably do a little spin.

Illus. 141

Experiment by bending up the trailing edges of the airplane's wings. You may want to slip a paper clip onto the fuselage just in back of the nose and see how that changes *Needle*'s flight path.

Now's a great time to think about designing your own paper airplanes. Keep in mind that many experimental folding designs don't work properly. When your plane fails, try to decide what went wrong. Are the wings too small to support the airplane in flight? Is the nose so light that the plane turns nose up instantly, or does it dive within 2' because the nose is too heavy?

After you figure out why a design doesn't fly perfectly, fold a new model that changes your experimental design. Don't give up, and don't feel bad when a design fails. Just go back to the drawing board and fold a better paper airplane next time!

ODDITIES

5.
Oddities

After folding some of the flying machines found in the four previous chapters, you may think that you've become an expert in odd flying machines. Some of the experimental models from the previous chapter are different from any plane that most people have folded and flown. *Gemini* certainly wasn't a common paper airplane, was it?

Although many of the airplanes you've already folded and flown were odd, the four fantastic paper flying machines in this chapter are *really* odd!

Airmail Heart

This is a great paper airplane to make for Valentine's Day. Of course, it will fly just as well on any other day.

Fold your sheet of notebook paper, copy paper, or other paper in half the long way. Now draw half of a heart, just as though you were going to make a big valentine heart. Check Illus. 142 before you begin to draw. Do you see how the half-heart nearly fills the half-sheet of paper?

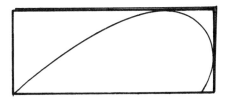

Illus. 142

Once you've drawn the half-heart, hold the two sides of the paper firmly together and cut around the line you just drew. Be sure the bottom layer of paper doesn't slip. If it does, you'll end up with a lopsided flying heart.

Once you've cut out the heart design, *Airmail Heart* should look much like the figure shown in Illus. 143. This drawing also shows a dotted fold line.

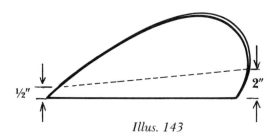

Illus. 143

See how the fold angles upwards, the closer to the airplane's tail it gets? Begin this fold about ½″ above the center fold at the nose of the plane. The fold should keep rising so that it's 2″ above the rear of the center fold. Check these measurements in Illus. 143 to see the relation to the folding you're about to do.

Now you're ready to fold. First fold the wing nearer to you. Glance at Illus. 144 to see how *Airmail Heart* will look once both wings have been folded.

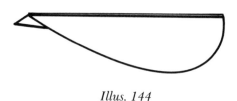

Illus. 144

See how the curved edge of the wing comes right down to the center fold? Now that you know how things should look, go ahead and fold both wings into place.

Slip a paper clip over the center fold about 1″ in back of the airplane's nose and launch the plane with a firm but gentle forward motion of your hand and arm. *Airmail Heart* should give you a smooth, easy glide path.

If you want to turn this odd paper flying machine into a true flying valentine, write a message on it. Illus. 145 shows how a Valentine's Day greeting might look.

Illus. 145

If you really want to be fancy, here's another idea. Remove the paper clip from the airplane's nose, and spread the wings a bit, as shown in Illus. 146.

Tape a small wrapped candy onto the fuselage, about 4″ back of the nose.

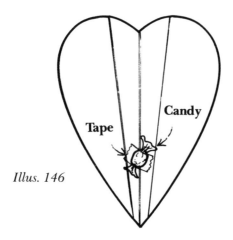

Illus. 146

Test your flying valentine to make certain that the candy is in the proper position to give your airplane the correct trim. You may need to move the candy forward or towards the rear of the fuselage in order to adjust the trim.

Your flying valentine will be welcomed as it flies to that special someone.

Soda-Straw Glider

This odd paper flying machine is probably completely unlike anything you've ever considered flying.

Begin with a piece of paper 3½″ wide by 6″ long. Fold it in half the long way, so that you end up with a slim piece of material that's 6″ long. The folded paper is shown in Illus. 147.

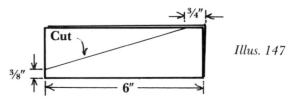

Illus. 147

Illus. 147 shows a cut line that begins about ⅜″ above the center fold on the left, and angles upward as the cut moves towards the right. Make this cut now.

When you unfold the paper you just cut, it should look like the drawing shown in Illus. 148.

Place a 7½″ soda straw right on top of the center fold so that the straw covers the fold. If your straw is longer than 7½″, cut it to the proper length. Illus. 149 shows that the end of the straw and the small end of the paper come right together.

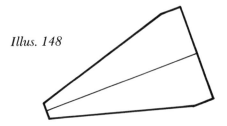

Illus. 148

As you can see in Illus. 149, there are three small strips of tape holding the straw firmly to the wing. When you apply these strips of tape, lift up the edges of the wings slightly. Press the tape into place so that it holds the straw to the wing and it also keeps the wing edges lifted upwards just a bit.

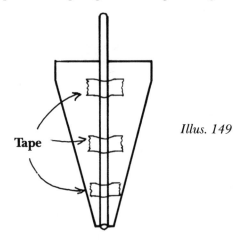

Tape

Illus. 149

Cut a piece of file-folder material 1¾″ by 3″. A piece of file card will work if you don't have any file-folder material left over.

Illus. 150 shows where to cut this rectangle of stiff material in half diagonally; make that cut now. You're going to use only one of the triangular pieces of material, but save the second piece to use if you decide to make another *Soda-Straw Glider*.

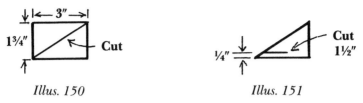

Illus. 150　　　　　　　*Illus. 151*

Illus. 151 shows the vertical stabilizer you just cut from stiff material, and the next bit of cutting ahead of you.

This cut should be about 1½″ long. Make certain the cut is parallel to the bottom of the vertical stabilizer and ¼″ from the bottom of the material.

Once this cut is made, make a 1½″ cut along the top of the soda straw. Illus. 152 shows this cut. Make sure you cut in a straight line at the very top of the straw.

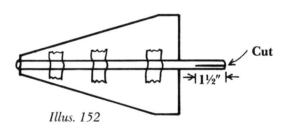

Illus. 152

As soon as you've made this cut, slip the vertical stabilizer into the end of the straw. Slide it all the way forward, so that it looks like the drawing shown in Illus. 153.

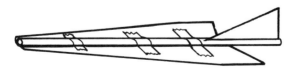

Illus. 153

Slip a paper clip onto the top of the straw at the airplane's nose, and slip a second paper clip onto the bottom of the straw at the same point. Be sure that the bottom clip goes over the paper wing when you do this. Illus. 154 shows these clips already in place.

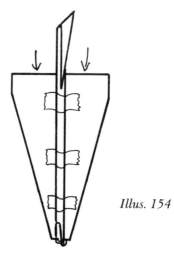

Illus. 154

Take a quick test flight. Hold the straw just in back of the wing between your thumb and your middle finger. The tip of your forefinger should rest on the end of the straw.

Your *Soda-Straw Glider* will probably do a nose dive. If it does, bend up the trailing edges of the wing just a bit. The arrows shown in Illus. 154 point to where you'll do this bending.

Adjust the wing's trailing edges until you have the proper trim. This glider won't fly great distances, but it should give a nice, even flight once you have it trimmed correctly.

If you want to experiment, why not make a *Soda-Straw Glider* using a longer straw? When you do that, you'll have to make the plane's wings longer and a bit wider than they are on the model you're making right now.

Flutter

Once you've folded *Flutter* there won't be any question in your mind about how this little flying machine got its name.

First cut a strip of paper 3″ wide and 11″ long from one side of a sheet of notebook paper or other paper.

Once you have that strip of paper, make the 5″ cut shown in Illus. 155.

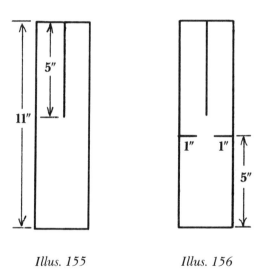

Illus. 155   Illus. 156

Make this 5″ cut exactly down the center of your paper strip.

Move on to Illus. 156. Measure up 5″ from the opposite end of the paper and mark the two cut lines shown in the drawing. Each of these lines is 1″ long. Once you've measured, make these two cuts.

Put away your scissors, and get ready to do some easy folding. As you can see in Illus. 157, make two folds. Fold over both sides of the paper along the dotted lines shown in the drawing.

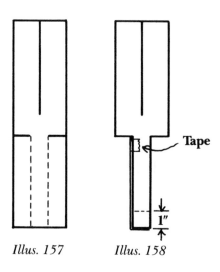

Illus. 157   *Illus. 158*

Now you're at Illus. 158. Wrap a small piece of tape around the folded part of *Flutter*, as shown in the drawing. After doing this, fold the bottom of the project along the little dotted line near the bottom of the drawing. Make this fold 1″ from the bottom of the material. Illus. 159 shows this fold in place.

Illus. 159 shows where to add another bit of tape to *Flutter*. This tape keeps the bottom fold from coming undone when *Flutter* does its thing.

There are two fold lines shown in Illus. 160, but don't fold yet. When you make these folds, fold one strip of paper towards you and fold the other away from you. This is important; otherwise *Flutter* won't flutter.

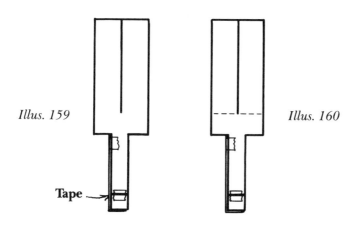

Illus. 159

Illus. 160

Tape

Illus. 161 gives you a side view of *Flutter* once this final folding is finished.

All that remains is to see how *Flutter* got its name. Hold it

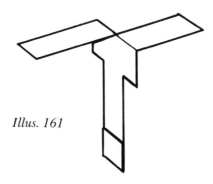

Illus. 161

high over your head and let it go. It will spin to the ground like a little helicopter, with its blades rotating and fluttering as it falls.

The farther *Flutter* has to fall, the longer it spins and flutters. That's all it does, but it's great fun to watch.

Try making smaller models of *Flutter* and see how they act. Stand on your porch and drop *Flutter* over the side, giving it ample room to fall. Just remember to rescue *Flutter* after each flight, otherwise *Flutter* just becomes litter, and no one likes that.

This is a great flying machine to make and use to entertain small children.

Whirler

At the beginning of this volume I mentioned that you'd need one of the big cardboard tubes which comes in the middle of a roll of gift-wrap paper. Now's the time you'll need a piece of one of those cardboard tubes.

You'll need a cardboard tube which is at least 2″ across. If you have a tube handy which is 2½″ in diameter or even a bit larger, that's great.

Very carefully, use your scissors to cut off one end of the cardboard tube, so that you have a cylinder which is a little over 3″ long. When you poke one blade of the scissors through the side of the tube it's easy to collapse the tube. A little bend won't matter because you can straighten it out, but there's a way to avoid bending the tube. Roll a newspaper and slip it into the tube, and then push the point of one scissor blade through the cardboard a little over 3″ from the end of the tube. You won't collapse the tube and (even better) you won't poke your finger with the scissors.

Have you seen my newspaper?

Once you have a cardboard cylinder that's a little more than 3″ long, stand it one end, so that it looks like the one shown in Illus. 162.

Slip four paper clips over the top end of the cylinder. Illus. 162 shows where to place the paper clips.

Next, wrap a strip of masking tape around the paper clips, so that your *Whirler* looks like the one shown in Illus. 163. It's fine if the ends of the masking tape overlap a bit. If you don't have masking tape, use cellophane tape. Masking tape is heavier than cellophane tape, and you'll be using the

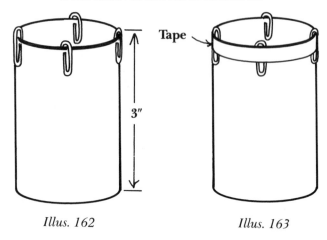

Illus. 162   *Illus. 163*

tape to add to *Whirler*'s nose weight, in addition to holding the paper clips in place.

Set aside this part of the project for a minute or two. Next, cut three pieces of file-folder material that are as long as your cardboard cylinder, and 1″ wide. You should end up with three pieces of stiff material about 3″ or so long and 1″ wide. If you don't have a bit of old file folder around, use an old file card.

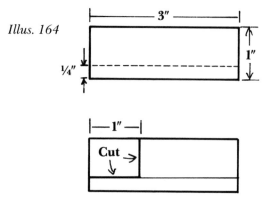

Fold each piece of material ¼″ from the edge, along the fold line shown in Illus. 164.

Once that fold is in place, flatten out the material, so that each piece looks like Illus. 165.

Illus. 165 shows two cut lines. The first runs along the fold for 1″. The second cut comes in from the side of the material until it meets the fold line. Make this pair of cuts in each of the three pieces of file-folder material.

When you've done this cutting, your three chunks of stiff material should look like those in Illus. 166.

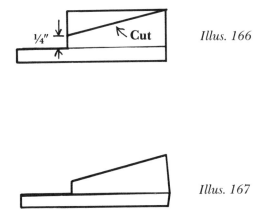

Illus. 166

Illus. 167

Your final cutting chore is shown by the cut line in Illus. 166. The cut angles itself from the right-hand corner of the material to a point ¼″ above the fold line. Make these cuts in all three pieces.

These three pieces of material will form the fins for *Whirler*.

Once you've finished cutting, refold each fin along the original fold line so that the two parts of the fin are at right angles to each other. The finished fin is shown in Illus. 167.

Now attach the fins to the body of this flying machine. Illus. 168 shows how one fin has been taped to the cardboard cylinder.

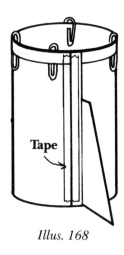

Illus. 168

Space the three fins evenly around the cylinder and tape all three onto the sides of the cardboard tube. Make certain each fin runs straight up the side of the tube.

Once you've taped all three fins in place, wrap another strip of tape (masking tape if you have it) around the ends of the fins to help hold them in place. Illus. 169 shows the tape wrapped around *Whirler*.

Take *Whirler* outside. Don't test this flying machine inside, since it has those paper clips, and because you're going to launch *Whirler* hard and fast. Of course if you can use the

I told you not to fly it in the house!

school gym, that's fine. Don't launch *Whirler* inside your bedroom or living room.

Whirler is launched underhand. Hold *Whirler* in your cupped hand, as shown in Illus. 170.

See how the weighted nose is towards the front of your hand. To launch *Whirler*, give a quick, hard forward movement of your entire arm. Let *Whirler* slide off your fingertips. You want this little flying machine to start spinning as it rolls off your fingertips. Give it a helping start by deliberately raising your hand as you launch *Whirler*.

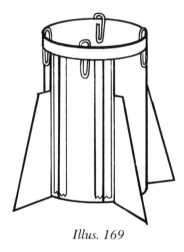

Illus. 169

Take it outside and try a few test flights to learn how to give *Whirler* a spinning motion, at the same time that you're swinging your hand and arm forward. It's not difficult.

When everything is working properly, *Whirler* will sail in an almost straight line for quite a distance. It can do this because it's spinning around and around, as though it had a little axle running right down the center of the hollow tube. It acts like a gyroscope as it spins through the air.

Illus. 170

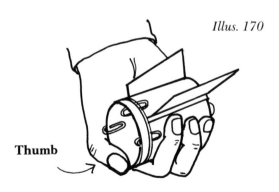

Thumb

If *Whirler* wants to tumble instead of flying straight, add another wrap of tape around its nose. Once you've got exactly the right amount of tape and you've mastered how to launch *Whirler*, this little flying machine will fly straight and true.

Just remember to give it lots and lots of spin when you launch it. The faster *Whirler* spins, the straighter it will fly.

Metric Equivalents

INCHES TO MILLIMETRES AND CENTIMETRES

MM—millimetres   CM—centimetres

Inches	MM	CM	Inches	CM	Inches	CM
⅛	3	0.3	9	22.9	30	76.2
¼	6	0.6	10	25.4	31	78.7
⅜	10	1.0	11	27.9	32	81.3
½	13	1.3	12	30.5	33	83.8
⅝	16	1.6	13	33.0	34	86.4
¾	19	1.9	14	35.6	35	88.9
⅞	22	2.2	15	38.1	36	91.4
1	25	2.5	16	40.6	37	94.0
1¼	32	3.2	17	43.2	38	96.5
1½	38	3.8	18	45.7	39	99.1
1¾	44	4.4	19	48.3	40	101.6
2	51	5.1	20	50.8	41	104.1
2½	64	6.4	21	53.3	42	106.7
3	76	7.6	22	55.9	43	109.2
3½	89	8.9	23	58.4	44	111.8
4	102	10.2	24	61.0	45	114.3
4½	114	11.4	25	63.5	46	116.8
5	127	12.7	26	66.0	47	119.4
6	152	15.2	27	68.6	48	121.9
7	178	17.8	28	71.1	49	124.5
8	203	20.3	29	73.7	50	127.0

Index

About the Author

E. Richard Churchill, born and raised in Colorado, received two degrees from the University of Northern Colorado. He then taught elementary and middle school, and acted as school librarian in Greeley, Colorado.

Author and co-author of more than forty books, most of which were written for children and young adults, he and his co-author wife, Linda, have also written more than one hundred educational projects.

Churchill and his wife travel in the U.S., and make yearly visits to Great Britain. Two dogs and a cat share their rural Colorado home.